Christmas Tra

The History Behind Christmas Traditions In America

Written By
Lynda M Lacroix

"A person can have no better epitaph than that which is inscribed in the hearts of his friends."
-Unknown

All rights reserved © 2010 Lynda M Lacroix.

Disclaimer and Terms of Use: While all attempts have been made to provide effective, verifiable information in this book, neither the Author nor Publisher assumes any responsibility for any errors, inaccuracies, or omissions. Any slights of people or organizations are unintentional.

If advice concerning financial matters is needed, the service of a qualified professional should be sought. This book is not a source of financial information and should not be used as such.

This publication is designed to provide accurate and authoritative information in regards to only the subject matter covered.

Table of Contents

Introduction	6
Where Christmas Began	9
How to Define A Christmas Tradition	17
Where Did The Traditions Start	21
Santa Claus	22
The Christmas Tree	28
Reading Christmas Stories	33
The Yule Log	34
Christmas Caroling	37
Gift Giving	40
Candy Canes	42
Christmas Cards	44
The Poinsettia	47
Conclusion	49

Introduction

There are many traditions that we follow or know about including: the Christmas tree, hanging stockings, Christmas cards, caroling, Santa Claus, gift giving, eggnog, and the Yule Log.

Do you know where any of these traditions came from? Are you someone that believes they've simply "always existed" and is something we, as a nation have always done every year around December 24th? Or do you believe that our family ancestors "created" these traditions?

If you believe either of these two lines of thought, then you really don't know much about the history of Christmas traditions. Have you ever wondered why we do the things we do when the days get shorter, the air becomes chilly, and the snow begins to fall.

There is a reason we perform every single Christmas tradition we know today and some of them may not be quite what you think! You will discover throughout these pages why certain Christmas traditions are performed every year and where exactly in the world they came from. Here's a secret you may not know. Many of the Christmas traditions we use to celebrate our National Holiday didn't even originate in the USA!

Do you find that hard to believe? Well, it's 100% without a doubt ... FACT. Christmas almost didn't exist in our country!

Yep, it's a true fact that some of the earliest "Powers That Be" did not believe in the Holiday because of its origins. You might be thinking, "How can that be? Surely that can't be the case at all and someone must be misinformed about this sacred holiday!"

I assure you that someone IS misinformed about this holiday. Would you like to know exactly where it all began and how we celebrate the Christmas holiday today? It is all a result of our past.

You're going to be able to read about the whole thing right here and now within these very pages so that you get to the bottom of things. So sit back, grab a cup of your favorite Holiday beverage, and prepare to discover...... **Christmas Traditions: The History Behind Christmas Traditions In America!**

Wishing You and Yours a Happy Holiday Season,

Lynda M. Lacroix
Belle Manor Farms

Where Christmas Began

Christmas. The word itself inspires feelings of joy and goodwill towards our fellow man. It was a day when the greatest gift in the entire world was bestowed upon us from Heaven.

When you think of the name "Christmas" you immediately think of the birth of Jesus Christ. Traditionally, that is what we believe is the reason behind the Christmas holiday and celebration, the birth of Jesus Christ. Even His name is in the word itself!

Is this really where the beginning of the Christmas holiday comes from? Or was it somewhere else? Would you believe it is rooted somewhere else? Let's go back to the time before Jesus Christ's birth, and see if we can't make sense of this. . . .

Centuries before Christ was born there was a group of people who celebrated something they called "The Winter

Solstice". In this celebration, early Europeans would gather together and rejoice that the worst part of the winter season had passed and they had managed to survive another harsh, cold winter. Also, they could begin enjoying longer days. In other words, this was a celebration of light itself... and life as well.

This celebration of light and survival would take place around December 21st or 22nd every year. Depending on the calendar shift, the celebration could occur sometime between the dates of December 20th up to the 23rd. This is pretty close to the time we traditionally celebrate our Christmas holiday, wouldn't you agree?

Indeed, all across the European countryside the end of December was an ideal time to have a celebration. Cattle were slaughtered to keep the farmers from having to feed throughout the entire winter. For a lot of people, this would be one of the few times throughout the entire year they would have access to fresh meat.

Along this same time period, most beverages consumed such as beer and wine which had been cultivated throughout the year, had finished the fermentation cycle and were ready to be consumed. Beer and burgers? Now if that doesn't sound like the makings of a party, I don't know what is!

Also during this time, many people in Germany would pay tribute to the pagan god Oden. Many Germans during this time who believed in this god were extremely afraid of him. They believed that Oden would make "nightly rounds" to check up on his people, deciding who would thrive and who would not. Because of this, many German people would stay indoors with their families.

Many different cultures celebrated this time of year. Not just the Winter Solstice and praising Oden, but Romans later celebrated Saturnalia, the god of agriculture. Can you guess what day his birthday was? **December 25th!**

As you can see, there are a lot of similarities in the way in which we celebrate Christmas. Small similarities, but they are still similar nonetheless. Even before Jesus Christ was born, we have groups of people in different countries celebrating around a specific time frame during the winter months.

Now let's discuss the birth of Jesus Christ.

It is believed by many through the words of the Holy Bible that Jesus Christ was born on or around December 25th. This would be his "Birthday". But, was it truly his Birthday?

In reality, no one has this finite answer. We can only assume that what we are reading is the truth, handed down through time to us. There are no "official" birth and death records for Jesus' time period so that we can go back and look at to see exactly when He was born. There is some evidence to suggest that His birth may have actually occurred earlier in the year than the winter season.

If you take a look at the Biblical evidence, it says that there were shepherds in the fields during the time Jesus was being delivered. If that were true, then He would not have been born during December as shepherds would not be herding their sheep in the middle of winter. Maybe they would and maybe they wouldn't. We don't know this for sure.

What we do know is this. . . . Jesus' actual birth date is not mentioned throughout the pages of the Bible. His death is which is why we celebrate Easter. In the earlier days of Christianity, Easter was the main holiday celebrated in relation to Jesus Christ. His birthday wasn't even celebrated at all!

It wasn't until the 4th century that Church officials declared Jesus Christ's birthday to be a celebrated holiday event. If no one knew what Jesus' actual birth date was, why would Pope Julius I have selected December 25th for it to be celebrated on?

Some historians believe this was done to try and dissolve the Saturnalia festival in early Roman times along with other pagan worship festivals that were frowned upon by the Church occurring around this time. Why were these celebrations "frowned" upon? Let's examine Saturnalia as an example.

During this celebration which lasted an entire week, Roman people would participate in all sorts of activities that included drinking and eating as much as they wanted. Basically they did as they pleased without recourse from any laws or authorities to themselves or others.

At the start of the festival, the Roman authoritative buildings would be shut down and Roman officials would select someone to represent the "Lord of Misrule". More often than not, this would be someone deemed as "an enemy of the Roman people", or a criminal for lack of a better term. In addition, each Roman community would do likewise within their individual communities.

The persons selected by their communities would then enjoy a week long binge of drinking, sex, and any indulgence they pleased. At the end of the week, the person selected as the "Lord of Misrule" would be executed as a way of combating "dark forces". It's pretty easy to see why the Church would want to do away with this type of celebration.

The Christmas celebration envisioned by the Church, or the celebration of Jesus Christ's birth, was appealing to many in its earliest form. Simply because it allowed different cultures to continue their celebrations as they normally did, but they celebrated them at a specific designated time..... December 25th.

In the years that followed, the Christmas celebration gained in popularity so much so that it extended all the way to places such as England by the end of the sixth century and Scandinavia by the end of the eighth century. Now Christmas, or some form of it, is celebrated worldwide.

Of course some cultures still reserve "Christmas" as a holiday season to celebrate the power of "light". Christians will argue that Jesus is but God's Holy "Light".

In all cultures, in some form or another, the Christmas holiday is a joyous celebration of life and goodness, which can also be seen as a celebration of "light". Even if the celebration may not be called "Christmas", the concepts are still rooted in the same historical religious ideas.

However, there were some Christians, like the Puritans, who didn't want to observe Jesus Christ's birthday as a holiday. They wouldn't allow their followers to treat it as a holiday either.

You may wonder about the reason. They did not believe that December 25th was in fact the birth date of their Savior, Jesus Christ. They believed the only reason this date was chosen to represent His birth was to create a worldwide celebration to conform all pagan religions over to Christianity. Therefore, it was not a date that the Puritans wanted to celebrate.

In fact some early Puritan American colonists completely banned the celebration of Christmas in Boston between the years 1659 and 1681 approximately. If you were caught in the act of celebrating such a pagan originated holiday, you would be fined for doing so.

There were other colonies that did take part in Christmas celebrations throughout early times in America and went against the grain. Due to the diligence and perseverance of a few, the Christmas we celebrate has survived throughout the long years. How do we go from celebrating Jesus Christ's birthday to stockings, Christmas trees, drinking eggnog, receiving gifts and all the commercialization elements of the holiday as we celebrate it today?

The part concerning the "gifts" is understandable to a point. Jesus was our "gift" from God or if you have different beliefs, our life is a "gift" from an ultimate source of power. But how does this correlate with getting an iPod?

In the next chapters, we'll find out what exactly what a "Christmas tradition" is and where many of our Christmas traditions come from.

How to Define a Christmas Tradition

In its simplest form, a tradition is something we do, either individually or collectively in a group, each and every year around or on a specific date or time. Because of this, we call it a tradition. It is something we do and everyone who knows us knows we do.... year in and year out... without fail.

In this instance of course, we're talking about Christmas as that specific time or date when we do these things. Therefore the term "Christmas Tradition" came about.

Some people may exchange presents between one another. Others may give gifts to those who are poverty stricken. Others may not give any store-bought gifts and have gift qualifications such as those that are only "hand-made" by their loved ones.

Many families have their own rich, historic, family traditions that go back generations while others make up their own for a new generation to enjoy. All traditions whether new or old, are practiced greatly upon what each individual family, or person, feels should be done.

Traditions can be simple or they can be complicated. For instance, every year you and your family decide there should be one new Christmas tree decoration purchased to mark that year. This helps to preserve that moment in time when your family was together and things were at their best.

In other cases, it can be a bit more complicated. Almost like a ceremony if you will. Take this example:

One family may have lost a dear loved one 2 days before Christmas or maybe even on Christmas. So every year before doing anything else, they drive out to visit the cemetery where their dearly departed has been placed. They purchase new flowers or a grave blanket and place it on the grave to pay their respects.

Maybe they have a family prayer or simply have a conversation with their loved one telling them all the things that happened throughout the course of the year. After the prayer they light a candle. This is a new tradition they will follow now each year. After this is over, they leave the cemetery and return home for a wonderful Christmas gathering to further celebrate the life of their loved one and also the birth of Jesus Christ.

Another tradition may be a person who doesn't regularly attend Church, or hasn't done so for years who goes to Church only on Christmas Eve or Christmas Morning.

The point is, a tradition is something that people do every year at the same time, no matter what that "something" is. In this case, that something we're speaking of is a Christmas tradition, which is something you specifically do around Christmas time.

This would be where things such as decorating the Christmas Tree, hanging stockings up, wrapping presents, visiting family and friends you don't normally see throughout the rest of the year, going sledding with your children, going to school plays or pageants, going Christmas caroling, collecting donations for local charitable organizations, making cookies or homemade candies, drinking eggnog, and so on come in to the picture.

Simple acts such as hanging up stockings and filling them with small gifts, fruit, nuts, or candy could be something you and your family do each year. This is one of your Christmas traditions that you follow based on an old hand-me-down tradition but you may have changed that tradition and customized it for your own family without even realizing it. Do you put only fruit and candy in the stockings? Or maybe small unwrapped toys? Or do you put a combination of things in the stockings?

Obviously, some things we do are steeped more in history than others. Every tradition has a history whether it's a new tradition or one that has been passed on from generation to generation. That's the most important part about Christmas traditions. The history of a tradition tells us why it's done. It's not really the act of doing them that makes them an integral part of our lives. It is the feeling we get by following the tradition.

You may wonder, "Why do I put up a Christmas tree every year?" It might seem silly to cut down a tree and bring it indoors for only a short time. There is history behind this tradition but it has adapted over the years. Many families choose to put up artificial trees to save our forests.

Where Did Traditions Start

In order to fully understand why, as American's, we perform different tasks throughout the celebration of Christmas, it is important to know where exactly each tradition originally came from.

Many Christmas traditions we perform during the holiday did not originate in America at all. Remember that the United States is the melting pot. When America was just an infant itself, it was comprised of many different peoples from many different countries.

These people had their own customs and traditions they carried right along with them to the new land. Over time, families from different cultures merged together and they merged their traditions. This is another reason why here in America, not everyone celebrates Christmas the same. Let's look at some of these traditions.

Santa Claus

The tradition of Santa Claus goes back centuries and is one of the reasons why we give gifts today. Santa Claus, as we know and love him today, didn't start out that way. It all began in the 4th century A.D. with a man by the name of St. Nicholas. What bridged the gap between modern day Santa Claus and the legend of St. Nicholas are his endearing acts of generosity.

It is said that in one particular act of kindness and generosity St. Nicholas saved the lives of three sisters. The story goes that three sisters were to be sold by their father into slavery or prostitution because he was a poor. He was a God fearing man but had no dowries to bestow upon his daughters to save them from a terrible future. St. Nicholas heard of this man and one night ventured off to his home.

Peering in the window, St. Nicholas saw the three sisters fast asleep in their bed. He noticed that they had just finished washing their stockings and had hung them to dry by the window and the fireplace.

As the story goes, St. Nicholas then took several gold pieces from his pocket and began throwing them through the window and down the chimney. Amazingly enough, the gold pieces fell into the stockings. When they awoke in the morning, they found their stockings filled with shimmering gold pieces that saving them from a destitute future.

That's just one of the many acts of charity St. Nicholas performed. It is the most well known and retold account. He performed many other everyday 'miracles' rescuing the poor from the fate that awaited them.

His legend spread throughout Europe like wildfire and hopeful children would leave their stockings hung beside the chimney. In some cultures, their wooden shoes were placed on the hearth. They would awake in the morning to find all sorts of presents and goodies filling their empty stockings or shoes.

It is of importance that Nicholas at the time he was performing these acts of kindness was not a Saint. He was an ordinary man with an extraordinary heart. He cared for his fellow man and was a devout follower of Christianity modeling his life around it. He ascended to

Sainthood because of his good deeds and acts of charity to the less fortunate.

St. Nicholas looked nothing like the Santa Claus we are familiar within today's American society however. This new vision of Santa came a long time after, but his character was based on the legendary St. Nicholas. What a wonderful person to base a figure after who is loved by children the world over!

Around the 17th century in Britain, there was a notoriously jolly man that delivered gifts to children across the country on Christmas Eve lovingly referred to as Father Christmas. He wasn't exactly our vision of Santa Claus, but it's pretty darn close.

Father Christmas was an older gentleman with a cheerful face. A somewhat portly fellow that had a white beard, and dressed in a green robe trimmed in white fur, carrying a staff. Basically, he looked like an older Christian fellow or maybe

'Gandalf" from the Lord of the Rings? Yeah. You get the picture. If you watch the classic Charles Dickens *A Christmas Carol* and spy the Ghost of Christmas Past, you'll see someone that is similar to what Father Christmas looked like with the white beard and hair of course.

How did Santa get his name?

Chalk that one up to the Dutch. People from the Netherlands also had created their own version of Santa. But to them, he was called by the name "Sinterklaas". Sounds a lot like "Santa Claus", right?

It doesn't end there with the Dutch though. Have you ever wondered where all of Santa's little helpers came from? Yep, I'm speaking about the elves. Well, those were a contribution from the Dutch too!

The story goes that St. Nicholas set free a little Ethiopian boy named "Piter" from a Myra marketplace where he was to serve indefinitely throughout his life. Because of this, Piter decided to devote his life to his savior, St. Nicholas, and help him out with his work.

Later on, the one "helper" became many and so we have Santa's helpers or his little elves that help Santa get ready for the biggest night of the year, Christmas Eve. On an interesting side note, "Piter" was given this name to represent another saint that went by the name of Peter. You may have heard of him, St Peter?

So now we know where Santa came from and how he got his name. But how did he go from the look of Father Christmas to jolly old Saint Nick?

This one is easy.

On December 23, 1823 a local newspaper called the *Sentinel* printed in Troy, New York, released a moving Christmas poem entitled *A Visit From St. Nicholas*. We know it today as *The Night Before Christmas*.

As we all know from our own childhood, Santa is portrayed as a portly old fellow with a red nose and cheeks, white beard, and fur trimmed outfit. We also know from the poem that Santa is equipped to do his nightly rounds with a sleigh and eight tiny reindeer.

Santa began donning the red outfit sometime later in 1863 when an American cartoonist by the name of Thomas Nast that appeared in *Harper's Weekly*. Since then Santa has been for the most part looking the same. Later on, in about 1885, Santa made his first appearance on a Christmas greeting card wearing his traditional red clothes and looking mainly as he does still to this very day.

The Christmas Tree

Besides a beautiful blanket of freshly fallen, glistening snow, Christmas Trees really make the holiday special. Each one has its own personality very much like snowflakes. No two people will decorate a tree the same.

But, did the tradition begin in America? Certainly not!

It actually began in Germany. In about the 8th century, there was a missionary that went by the name of Winfred. Later in life this man attained Sainthood and was called St. Boniface. As the story goes, St. Boniface happened to run across a group of pagan worshipers near an oak tree. They were in the process of making a human sacrifice by means of a small boy to their god Thor.

Enraged by what he saw, St. Boniface chopped down the oak tree immediately. Once the tree was down, St. Boniface noticed that a tiny fir tree had miraculously sprung up in its place! At that time and forever after, the image of the fir tree was a symbol of Christianity and one of everlasting life.

Not until the 16th century did bringing a living tree indoors become a tradition. There is much speculation as to who exactly this tradition is accredited to. But, here is one scenario.

Around the year 1500 while walking home one winter evening, a man by the name of Martin Luther saw an amazing sight. Some say this winter evening was Christmas Eve. He came across a small patch of evergreen trees in the woods covered with freshly fallen snow that seemed to twinkle in the moonlight.

Martin Luther thought this was such a beautiful sight and he wished to share the story with his family. Thus, Martin Luther cut down a small fir tree, took it into his home, and decorated it with small, lit candles tied to the branches to recreate what he saw.

It is believed that the lighting of the candles was to simulate the stars that shone in the night sky, just as they had done during the first Christmas Eve over the small town of Bethlehem.

That was the earliest documented case of the indoor Christmas tree. In the story of Martin Luther, more people give him credit for decorating the first Christmas tree, however.

From 1500 or so up until around 1700, the custom of the indoor Christmas tree was growing in certain areas of Germany. After the year 1700 or thereabouts, adding lights and decorations such as apples etc., really made this custom take off and placed it into "tradition" status quickly across the land.

It is even rumored that during the Revolutionary War of 1776 in what is now more commonly known as Trenton, New Jersey, the Hessian soldiers left their posts to celebrate with thoughts of home around a candlelit evergreen tree on Christmas Eve. Because of this, they were defeated by George Washington and his troops.

Around 1848, Prince Albert presented England's Queen Victoria with the gift of a Christmas tree from. It's important to note that Price Albert was of Germanic descent and therefore, having an indoor decorated tree would be more traditional to him. This is also an example of mixing cultures and traditions.

When the people saw the sight of this gorgeously decorated and glowing indoor tree, they decided that they would like one too. It's sort of like 'keeping up with the Jones' thing. Thus more and more homes across England began including the "royal" tradition of a Christmas tree into the holiday season.

Eventually, the tradition of an indoor, freshly cut, and decorated Christmas tree became a part of our own American Tradition and was commonplace by the 1960's. Since then, the Christmas tree has become a symbol of the American Christmas holiday traditions long steeped in far off culture.

Reading Christmas Stories

This is a tradition many people follow today which started many years ago as moms read their children to sleep at night. But Americans did change this tradition for Christmas when a New York newspaper released the poem *A Visit From St. Nicholas* in 1823.

This poem was read to children before going to bed on Christmas Eve and later became a book published and shared around the world.

Maybe this is one of your holiday traditions. There are many Christmas story books published today that we read to the children during the holidays.

The Yule Log

The Yule Log, as we have come to know it, is a rather large piece of wood, cylindrical in shape, placed inside the fireplace and burned on Christmas Eve.
Or, you may know it simply as a little cake that resembles a wooden log!

Either way, they both originated from the same place, Northern Europe. While different regions would make use of the Yule Log in various ways, it was always used as part of Christmas Eve festivities.

More often than not, the Yule Log was brought inside, lit in the hearth, and kept burning from 12 hours to 12 days. This could be where the 12 days of Christmas idea came from.

During the Yule burning ritual, it was believed that a household would enjoy good luck in one form or another to every member of the home that the warmth of the fire from the Yule Log touched. Normally this meant a life full of health, wealth, and happiness.

It was also considered a tribute to Odin, the Norse god of war, wisdom, and death. And, in Scandinavian culture, the name of Odin was actually Jolnir. It is interesting to note that the first three letters in the aforementioned name was also the name of a popular Solstice festival and when pronounced it sounds like "Yule".

This tradition finally made its way to England, where the gathering of the Yule Log was an entire family event. Family members would venture out into the forest, select a huge tree, chop it down, make one great log from a portion of it, and drag it with ropes back to their home. The log had to be big enough to keep ablaze for 12 days.

It was widely believed that if you participated in the dragging, you would have good luck throughout the following year.

After the log had finished its burning cycle, a small bit of it was saved back for lighting next year's Yule Log. Some of the ashes from the Yule Log were scattered throughout the home owner's fields to ensure a healthy crop the following year.

This tradition made its way over to America from our English forefathers when they arrived to our country and has been part of our Christmas traditions ever since.

Christmas Caroling

The actual invention of Christmas caroling is not clear. Some claim that carols, derived from the French word Carole, meaning "kind of dance", began as far back as the 4th or 5th century A.D. Others report that carols, as we know them today, originated between the 12th and 13th centuries with St. Francis of Assisi, a Roman Catholic saint leading the way.

Because the act of caroling is an unwritten tradition, it makes the task of origination all the more difficult.

As the term "Carole" or "carol" implies, in the beginning, there were no Christian ties involved whatsoever. When one would "carol" in early times, they would be performing a traditional cultural dance often times accompanied by some sort of music. In the French translation of the word it is accompanied with song. In the early stages, there was no singing associated with the dancing.

What is known is that St Francis of Assisi ushered in a better known form of caroling by combining singing Christian songs or hymns with Christmas church services. But where did these hymns come from? It is believed that they were written around the 4th or 5th century A.D. praising the birth of Jesus Christ.

But why do Christmas carolers travel in groups going from house to house singing and celebrating the season today?

It is believed that this portion of Christmas caroling developed in or around the 16th century with those too poor "singing for their supper", going from door-to-door until they received enough food and drink to sustain them for the night.

The Christmas carol as we know it today wasn't widely accepted in America until the late 19th century, when it was concurrently made popular in England during the Victorian era.

There are still groups in some neighborhoods that get together and go 'caroling'. In some rural areas, farmers hitch up a wagon load of hay for a hayride and the passengers bundle up for the ride through the neighborhood, caroling and sharing the joy of Christmas.

Gift Giving

Logically, for most Christians, the act of gift giving would be symbolic of the first Christmas Eve and the Three Wise Men bestowing gifts upon the Virgin Mary and baby Jesus to celebrate his birth.

And indeed, this is where the tradition of gift giving began. Of course, throughout the ages and throughout countless civilizations such as the Romans and Egyptians, subjects would offer up gifts during ancient celebrations or festivals.

Unless you are a historian, or scholar, you would not be aware of these celebrations.

While the concept of gift-giving remains the same, the methods have changed quite a bit over the centuries. From the Victorian era on, gifts or presents, have been wrapped with elaborate papers, ribbons, and bows. Instead of placing the gifts at the foot of a King, they are now scattered underneath a Christmas Tree or found snuggled within our Christmas Stockings. Some traditions find the presents literally on the tree.

Even though some might lose sight of where the tradition of gift giving began, the messages these gifts bring forth are that of wonder, happiness, and love.

The Candy Cane

Would you believe that the Candy Cane as we are familiar with it today was actually invented as a tool to keep children quiet? It's true!

Back in the 1670's, a choirmaster at the Cologne Cathedral in Germany took a well known candy, a "sugar stick", and bent one end to resemble that of a Shepherd's staff to give to unruly children in order to keep them quiet during the long church Christmas ceremonies. This new idea quickly spread over to America and churches then began performing the same tradition within their midst.

Candy Canes, in their infancy, were mostly reserved for Christmas themed religious ceremonies. There was one documented case of someone decorating their Christmas Tree with the traditional "white" candies.

A man by the name of August Imgard, a German immigrant, displayed candy canes on his family Christmas tree in Wooster, Ohio, in the year 1847.

At first, the Candy Canes were all white, void of any other color. Until in the 1920's, a man by the name of Bob McCormack began making the Candy Cane as we know it today, with the red stripes included, for his family, neighbors, and friends. Bob did this process, every year all by hand.

That all changed when his brother in law, a Catholic priest by the name of Gregory Keller, invented a machine that automated the Candy Cane creation process in about 1950.

Now we all enjoy Candy Canes from the traditional red and white striped peppermint candies down to the multi colored fruity flavored ones.

The Christmas Card

No, Hallmark didn't start the Christmas card tradition. It was an English man by the name of Sir Henry Cole in 1843. Sir Henry needed a way to send out Christmas cards to family and friends to help the not so fortunate souls. Writing each one out by hand would be a tedious and timely task.

To save time, he hired a guy by the name of John Calcott Horsley to pick up the process. John set off to work and began hand painting an image onto a card that depicted the act of celebrating a joyous Christmas with family.

Under the picture read a caption that said, "A Merry Christmas and a Happy New Year to You". The idea wasn't one that inspired Sir Henry's friends and family to join in on his crusade and he didn't send any more cards out the following year. The idea of sending holiday wishes and greetings did catch on and spread rapidly.

Kate Greenaway, a prominent Victorian children's book writer and illustrator, assisted with the help of Frances Brundage and Ellen Clapsaddle, designed the first popular Christmas cards during the late 1800's into the early 1900's.

Thirty years or so after this, Americans that wanted Christmas cards to send out to family and friends had to import them from England. So England is held responsible for the creation and tradition of the Christmas card.

In 1875 a German immigrant by the name of Louis Prang started his very own lithography shop within the United States. At first, Louis didn't create traditional looking Christmas cards that we're familiar with today. As more people requested wintery scenes and Christmas tidings, Louis came up with some of the most beautiful designs ever spied with the human eye. By 1881 Louis was creating better than 5 million Christmas cards every year!

Today, we can find all sorts of different Christmas cards sporting every Christmas greeting imaginable in shops all across the U.S. (including Hallmark).

Many today, like to use their imagination and make personalized Christmas cards from paper, ribbon, and old pictures they have at home. This not only sends out a message of joy and goodwill to friends and family, but also shows the recipient you care enough to take the time and make a personalized cared.

Not everyone is into automation and commercialization. Remember, Christmas can be what you make it to be.

The Poinsettia

After reading that most of our American holiday traditions stemmed from Europe you would think it would only stand to reason that the tradition of placing Poinsettia flowers around our homes would also come from that region.

Well, if you thought that, you would be 100% Wrong! Actually, this tradition came all the way from Mexico!

Our American tradition of displaying Poinsettias around our homes was the brain child of none other than Joel Roberts Poinsett. Check out the name! You knew what was coming.

If it were not for the love of botany by Joel R. Poinsett, we may have never even known about this beautiful and festive flower at all. In 1825, Joel R. Poinsett was appointed to the prestigious title of the United States Ambassador to Mexico.

On one of his journeys to Mexico, he discovered the vibrantly red flower. He immediately fell in love with it as a practicing botanist and shipped some of them back to his home in Greenville, South Carolina.

After a short time of cultivating the flowers inside his hothouses, he began sending them to his friends and family as a Christmas gift. These beautiful flowers made wonderful living gifts as well as beautiful decorations for the Christmas holidays.

Now we display them within our own homes and can purchase them from any greenhouse or corner shop.

Conclusion

While few of the traditions we celebrate as a part of our American Christmas began in our country, each tradition was meaningful to the culture that created them. They are just as meaningful to us today even if the meaning may be somewhat different.

One thing is clear, Christmas is a joyous occasion that we spend with family and friends not only to celebrate the birth of Jesus Christ, but to enjoy one another's company if only for one day out of the year.

It is my sincere hope that you have enjoyed reading about where our American Christmas traditions originated from and that you remember, even though we may come from different places around the globe, we are all connected as brothers and sisters.

Wishing You A Happy & Healthy Holiday,

Lynda M. Lacroix
Belle Manor Farms

Printed in Great Britain
by Amazon